GENERAL SYNTAX

FORMAT

- Spaces, Tabs, Newlines, and Formfeeds are used as separators. Extra such characters are legal and can be used to improve code format.
- It is suggested that you indent code with Tabs for readability.

COMMENTS

- Begin with /*, end with */.
- Legal anywhere a Space is legal.
- *Examples* — • /* In-line comment */
  - • /*
      * Header comment
      */

D0223812

IDENTIFIERS

- Identifiers are used as the names of variables, functions, and data types.

- *Legal Characters* — *a-z A-Z 0-9* Underscore (_)
  - First character cannot be a digit.
  - An identifier may be more than 8 characters long, but on some systems not all characters are significant to the compiler and loader (see table below).
  - *Examples* — NAME1 name1 Total_5 Paper

- *External Identifiers* — Length and case requirements may vary even on the same computer, depending on the compiler and loader being used. *Note* — The industry standard for future *C* compilers is expected to be greater than 8 characters, all significant.
  - 3B* Computer   8 characters, 2 cases
  - DEC PDP-11   7 characters, 2 cases
  - DEC VAX-11   7 characters, 2 cases
  - HONEYWELL 6000   6 characters, 1 case
  - IBM 360/370   7 characters, 1 case
  - INTERDATA 8/32   8 characters, 2 cases
  - MOTOROLA 68000   >8 characters, 2 cases
  - NSC 16000   >8 characters, 2 cases
  - ZILOG 8000   >8 characters, 2 cases
  - INTEL 80286   >8 characters, 2 cases

  DEC, PDP, and VAX are trademarks of Digital Equipment Corporation.
  HONEYWELL, IBM, INTERDATA, MOTOROLA, NSC, ZILOG, and INTEL are trademarks of the respective companies.

---

*3B is a trademark of AT&T Technologies

RESERVED KEYWORDS

DATA TYPES	STORAGE CLASSES	STATEMENTS
char	auto	break
double	extern	case
enum	register	continue
float	static	default
int		do
long		else
short		for
struct		goto
union		if
unsigned		return
void		switch
		while
sizeof		
typedef		

Note — **sizeof** is an operator. **typedef** is used to define a shorthand form for an existing data type. Some implementations also reserve the words **asm** and **fortran**.

BASIC DATA TYPES

INTRODUCTION

The basic data types are integer (*int, short, long, unsigned*), character (*char*), and floating point (*float, double*). Other data types can be derived from these. (See *DECLARATIONS* on page 29.)

This section presents the syntax for constants, and for machine data sizes.

INTEGER CONSTANTS

Decimal
- Digits *0-9*.
- *First* digit must *not* be *0*.
- *Examples* — 12 111 956   1007
- *Note* — If value exceeds largest *signed* machine integer, it is taken to be *long*.

Octal
- Digits *0-7*.
- Prefixed by *0*.
- *Examples* — 012   —   10 Decimal
  0111   —   73 Decimal
  076   —   62 Decimal
  0123 — 1*64 + 2*8 + 3 — 83 Decimal
- *Note* — If value exceeds largest *unsigned* machine integer, it is taken to be *long*.

Hex
- Digits *0-9*, plus letters *a-f* or *A-F* for values *10-15*.
- Prefixed by *0x* or *0X*.
- *Examples* — 0x12   —   18 Decimal
  0X12   —   18 Decimal
  0x2f   —   47 Decimal
  0XA3   —   163 Decimal
  0x1B9 — 1*256 + 11*16 + 9 — 441 Decimal
- *Note* — If value exceeds largest *unsigned* machine integer, it is taken to be *long*.

LONG INTEGER CONSTANTS

- An *L* or *l* suffix explicitly specifies a *long* integer constant.

- *Examples* —

Decimal	12l	—	12	Decimal
	956L	—	956	Decimal
Octal	012l	—	10	Decimal
	076L	—	62	Decimal
Hex	0x12l	—	18	Decimal
	0XA3L	—	163	Decimal

FLOATING POINT CONSTANTS

- Always double-precision, that is, type *double*.

- Consists of —
  - Integer part — sequence of digits.
  - Decimal point.
  - Fraction part — sequence of digits.
  - *e* or *E*.
  - Integer Exponent (may be signed).

- One, but not both, of each of the following pairs may be omitted —
  - Integer *or* Fraction part.
  - Decimal point *or* e (*E*) and Integer Exponent.

- *Examples* —

345.	—	345	Decimal
3.14159	—	3.14159	Decimal
2.1E5	—	210000	Decimal
.123E3	—	123	Decimal
4037e−5	—	.04037	Decimal

CHARACTER CONSTANTS

- *One* ASCII character surrounded by *single* quotes (apostrophe). (See *CHARACTER SET* on page 76.)

- *Examples* — ´A´ ´a´ ´7´ ´$´

- *Special character constants* —

Newline (Linefeed)	NL (LF)	´\n´
Horizontal Tab	HT	´\t´
Vertical Tab	VT	´\v´
Backspace	BS	´\b´
Carriage Return	CR	´\r´
Formfeed	FF	´\f´
Backslash	\	´\\´
Single Quote	´	´\´´
Double Quote	"	´\"´
Null Character	NUL	´\∅´

  In addition, any character can be represented as a 3 digit octal code —

Octal Code	´\ddd´

- *Note* — The type of a character constant is integer (*int*).

STRING CONSTANTS

- A sequence of ASCII characters surrounded by *double* quotes ("...").

- *Examples* —
  - "This is a character string"
  - "THIS IS A CHARACTER STRING"
  - "A"
  - "1234567890"
  - "∅"
  - "$"

- Has type "array of characters" (*char []*) initialized with the given characters.

- The compiler places a null byte, \∅, at the end of each string to indicate the end.

- Every string constant, even if identical to other string constants, is stored at a *unique* location in memory.

- Within a string, if a double quote (") is used, it must be preceded by \. The other \'ed special character constants shown under *CHARACTER CONSTANTS* can also be used.

- A \ and an immediately following Newline are ignored.

ENUMERATION CONSTANTS

Names declared as enumerators behave like *int* constants. (See *DECLARATIONS* on page 29.)

HARDWARE DEPENDENT DATA SIZES

The following chart gives the sizes in bits of basic data types for various machines.

	3B Computer ASCII	DEC PDP-11 ASCII	DEC VAX ASCII
char	8 bits	8 bits	8 bits
int	32	16	32
short	16	16	16
long	32	32	32
float	32	32	32
double	64	64	64
float range	$\pm 10^{\pm 38}$	$\pm 10^{\pm 38}$	$\pm 10^{\pm 38}$
double range	$\pm 10^{\pm 308}$	$\pm 10^{\pm 38}$	$\pm 10^{\pm 38}$
byte order*	0123	10 32	3210

	HONEYWELL 6000 ASCII	IBM 360/370 EBCDIC	INTERDATA 8/32 ASCII
char	9 bits	8 bits	8 bits
int	36	32	32
short	36	16	16
long	36	32	32
float	36	32	32
double	72	64	64
float range	$\pm 10^{\pm 38}$	$\pm 10^{\pm 76}$	$\pm 10^{\pm 76}$
double range	$\pm 10^{\pm 38}$	$\pm 10^{\pm 76}$	$\pm 10^{\pm 76}$
byte order*	0123	0123	

Note — The following information was Preliminary at the time of publication of this handbook.

	MOTOROLA 68000 ASCII	NSC 16000 ASCII	ZILOG 8000 ASCII	INTEL 80286 ASCII
char	8 bits	8 bits	8 bits	8 bits
int	32**	32	16**	16
short	16	16	16	16
long	32	32	32	32**
float	32	32	32	32
double	32	64	64**	64
float range	$\pm 10^{\pm 38}$	$\pm 10^{\pm 38}$	$\pm 10^{\pm 38}$	$\pm 10^{\pm 38}$
double range	$\pm 10^{\pm 38}$	$\pm 10^{\pm 308}$	$\pm 10^{\pm 308}$	$\pm 10^{\pm 308}$
byte order*	0123	3210	01 23	32 10

---

* **byte order** — Address for the word starts at byte 0.

** To be determined

OPERATORS AND EXPRESSIONS

EXPRESSIONS

- An *expression* consists of one or more operands with an operator.
  - *Examples* —
    - a++
    - b = 10
    - x = (y*z)/w

- *Note* — An expression followed by a semicolon would be a *statement*. (See page 20.)

OPERAND NOTATION

- Some operators require specific kinds of operands. The following notation is used to indicate differences.
  - *e* — Any expression.
  - *v* — Any expression that refers to a variable to which a value can be assigned. Such expressions are called *lvalue* expressions.

- A *prefix* indicates expression type. For example, *ie* is any integer expression. The complete list of type prefixes follows.
  - *i* — integer or character
  - *a* — arithmetic (integer, character, or floating point)
  - *p* — pointer
  - *s* — structure or union
  - *sp* — structure or union pointer
  - *f* — function
  - *fp* — function pointer

  The notation *smem* indicates a structure or union member name.

- *Note* — If several operands appear in an expression, then they may be distinguished by appending numbers, for example, *ae1* + *ae2*.

ARITHMETIC

+

- *Usage*: *ae1* + *ae2*
  Sum of *ae1* and *ae2*.
- *Example*: i = j + 2;
  Set *i* equal to the value of *j* plus *2*.

- *Usage*: *pe* + *ie*
  Address *ie* variables beyond address given
  by *pe*. Type of variable is implied by type of
  pe.
- *Example*: last = arname + arsize − 1;
  Set *last* to the address of the last element of
  the array *arname*.

−

- *Usage*: *ae1* − *ae2*
  Difference of *ae1* and *ae2*.
- *Example*: i = j − 3;

- *Usage*: *pe* − *ie*
  Address *ie* variables before address given by
  pe.
- *Example*: first = last − arsize + 1;

- *Usage*: *pe1* − *pe2*
  Number of variables from *pe2* to *pe1*.
- *Example*: arsize = last − first;

−

- *Usage*: −*ae*
  Minus *ae*.
- *Example*: x = −x;

*

- *Usage*: *ae1* * *ae2*
  Product of *ae1* and *ae2*.
- *Example*: z = 3 * x;

/

- *Usage*: *ae1* / *ae2*
  Quotient of *ae1* divided by *ae2*.
- *Example*: i = j / 5;

%

- *Usage*: *ie1* % *ie2*
  Remainder of *ie1* divided by *ie2*, that is,
  ie1 modulo *ie2*.
- *Example*: minutes = time % 60;

Note — Side effects occur for the ++ and --
operators. That is, the value of the variable
which appears as the operand is changed.

++ • *Usage*: *iv*++
   Increment *iv* by 1. Value of the expression is
   iv before increment.
   • *Example*: j = i++;

• *Usage*: *pv*++
   Increment *pv* by 1 to point to the next object.
   Value of the expression is
   pv before increment.
   • *Example*: *ptr++ = 0;
   Assign value *0* to the variable pointed to by
   ptr, then increment *ptr* to point to the next
   variable.

• *Usage*: ++*iv*
   Increment *iv* by 1. Value of the expression is
   iv after increment.
   • *Example*: i = ++j;

• *Usage*: ++*pv*
   Increment *pv* by 1. Value of the expression
   is that of *pv after* increment.
   • *Example*: *++ptr = 0;

-- • *Usage*: *iv*--
   Decrement *iv* by 1. Value of the expression
   is *iv before* decrement.
   • *Example*: j = i--;

• *Usage*: *pv*--
   Decrement *pv* by 1 to point to the previous
   object. Value of the expression is
   pv before decrement.
   • *Example*: arrpos = p--;

• *Usage*: --*iv*
   Decrement *iv* by 1. Value of the expression
   is *iv after* decrement.
   • *Example*: i = --j;

• *Usage*: --*pv*
   Decrement *pv* by 1. Value of the expression
   is *pv after* decrement.
   • *Example*: prepos = --p;

ASSIGNMENT

Note — The value of an assignment expression
is the value of the left operand **after** the assignment.

=
- **Usage**: *v = e*
  Assign the value of *e* to *v*.
- **Example**: x = y;

Note — The following operators combine an
arithmetic or bitwise operation with assignment.

+=
- **Usage**: *av += ae*
  Increment *av* by *ae*.
- **Example**: y += 2;
  Increment *y* by 2.

- **Usage**: *pv += ie*
  Increment *pv* by *ie*.
- **Example**: p += n;

−=
- **Usage**: *av −= ae*
  Decrement *av* by *ae*.
- **Example**: x −= 3;

- **Usage**: *pv −= ie*
  Decrement *pv* by *ie*.
- **Example**: ptr −= 2;

*=
- **Usage**: *av *= ae*
  Multiply *av* by *ae*.
- **Example**: timesx *= x;

/=
- **Usage**: *av /= ae*
  Divide *av* by *ae*.
- **Example**: x /= 2;

%=
- **Usage**: *iv %= ie*
  Set *iv* to *iv* modulo *ie*.
- **Example**: x %= 10;

>>=
- **Usage**: *iv >>= ie*
  Shift *iv* right by *ie* bits.
- **Example**: x >>= 4;

<<=
- **Usage**: *iv <<= ie*
  Shift *iv* left by *ie* bits.
- **Example**: x <<= 1;

&=
- **Usage**: *iv &= ie*
  "And" *iv* with *ie*.
- **Example**: remitems &= mask;

`^=`
- *Usage*: *iv* `^=` *ie*
  Exclusive "or" *iv* with *ie*.
- *Example*: control `^=` seton

`|=`
- *Usage*: *iv* `|=` *ie*
  "Or" *iv* with *ie*.
- *Example*: additems `|=` mask;

RELATIONAL

Note — The logical value "false" is represented
by integer 0, and "true" by any non-zero value.
The values of relational and boolean
expressions are 0 for false and 1 for true.

`==`
- *Usage*: *ie1* `==` *ie2*
  True if *ie1* is equal to *ie2*; otherwise false.
- *Example*: if (i `==` 0)
         break;

- *Usage:* *pe1* `==` *pe2*
  True if the values of *pe1* and *pe2* are equal.

`!=`
- *Usage*: *ie1* `!=` *ie2*
  True if *ie1* is *not* equal to *ie2*.
- *Example*: while (i `!=` 0)
         i = func;

- *Usage*: *pe1* `!=` *pe2*
  True if the values of *pe1* and *pe2* are *not*
  equal.
- *Example*: if (p `!=` q)
         break;

`<`
- *Usage*: *ae1* `<` *ae2*
  True if *ae1* is less than *ae2*.
- *Example*: if (x `<` 0)
         printf ("negative");

- *Usage*: *pe1* `<` *pe2*
  True if the value of *pe1*, which is an address,
  is less than the value of *pe2*.
- *Example*: while (p `<` q)
         *p++ = 0;
  While the address given by *p* is less than the
  address given by *q*, assign 0 to the variable
  that *p* points to and increment *p* to point to
  the next contiguous variable.

<=
- *Usage*: *ae1* <= *ae2*
  True if *ae1* is less than or equal to *ae2*.

- *Usage*: *pe1* <= *pe2*
  True if *pe1* is less than or equal to *pe2*.

>
- *Usage*: *ae1* > *ae2*
  True if *ae1* is greater than *ae2*.
- *Example*: if (x > 0)
               printf ("positive");

- *Usage*: *pe1* > *pe2*
  True if the value of *pe1*, which is an address,
  is greater than the value of *pe2*.
- *Example*: while (p > q)
                *p–– = 0;

>=
- *Usage*: *ae1* >= *ae2*
  True if *ae1* is greater than or equal to *ae2*.

- *Usage*: *pe1* >= *pe2*
  True if the value of *pe1* is greater than or
  equal to *pe2*.

BOOLEAN

!
- *Usage*: *!ae* or *!pe*
  True if *ae* or *pe* is false.
- *Example*: if (!good)
               printf ("not good");

||
- *Usage*: *e1* || *e2*
  Logical "or" of *e1* and *e2*. *e1* is evaluated
  first, and *e2* is evaluated *only* if *e1* is false.
  Value is true if either *e1* or *e2* is true.
- *Example*: if (x < A || x > B)
               printf ("out of range");

&&
- *Usage*: *e1* && *e2*
  Logical "and" of *e1* and *e2*. *e1* is evaluated
  first, and *e2* is evaluated *only* if *e1* is true.
  Value is true only if both *e1* and *e2* are true.
- *Example*: if (p != NULL && *p > 7)
                 n++;
  If *p* is not a null pointer and the value of the
  variable pointed to by *p* is greater than *7*,
  increment *n*. Note that if the value of *p* is
  NULL (0), the expression **p* is nonsense.

BITWISE

~
- *Usage:* ~*ie*
  One's complement of *ie*. Value contains a 1
  in each bit position where *ie* contains a 0,
  and a 0 in each bit position where *ie* contains
  a 1.
- *Example*: opposite = ~mask;

>>
- *Usage*: *ie1* >> *ie2*
  ie1 shifted right by *ie2* bits. Right shifting
  may be arithmetic (that is, filled with sign bit)
  or logical, depending on the implementation;
  however, when applied to an unsigned
  integer, it is guaranteed to be logical and 0-
  filled on left.
- *Example*: x = x >> 3;

<<
- *Usage*: *ie1* << *ie2*
  ie1 shifted left by *ie2* bits and 0-filled on
  right.
- *Example*: fourx = x << 2;

&
- *Usage*: *ie1* & *ie2*
  Bitwise "and" of *ie1* and *ie2*. Value contains
  a 1 in each bit position where there is a 1 in
  both *ie1* and *ie2*, and a 0 in every other bit
  position.
- *Example*: flag = ((x & mask) != 0);

|
- *Usage*: *ie1* | *ie2*
  Bitwise "or" of *ie1* and *ie2*. Value contains a
  1 in each bit position where there is a 1 in
  either *ie1* or *ie2*, and a 0 in every other bit
  position.
- *Example*: attrsum = attr1 | attr2;

^
- *Usage*: *ie1* ^ *ie2*
  Bitwise exclusive "or" of *ie1* and *ie2*. Value
  contains a 1 in each bit position where there
  is a 1 in either *ie1* or *ie2*, but not both, and a
  0 in every other bit position.
- *Example*: diffbits = x ^ y;

ADDRESS

&
- *Usage*: **&v**
  Address of **v**.
- *Example*: intptr = &n;

*
- *Usage:* ***pe**
  Variable addressed by **pe**.
- *Example*: *ptr = c;

- *Usage:* ***fpe**
  Function pointed to by **fpe**.
- *Example*: fpe = funcname;
            (*fpe) (arg1, arg2);

ARRAY

[]
- *Usage*: **pe[ie]**
  A variable at offset **ie** variables from the address given by **pe**. Equivalent to ***(pe + ie)**.
- *Example*: arname[i] = 3;
  Assign the value **3** to element **i** of array **arname**. Note that the **first** element of an array would be given by **arname[0]**.

STRUCTURE/UNION

.
- *Usage*: **sv.smem**
  Member **smem** of structure or union **sv**.
- *Example*: product.p_revenue = 50;
  Assign the value **50** to the **p_revenue** member of a structure variable **product**.

−>
- *Usage*: **spe −> smem**
  Member **smem** of structure or union pointed to by **spe**. Equivalent to **(*spe).smem**
- *Example*: prodptr −>p_revenue = 2;
  Assign the value **2** to the **p_revenue** member of the structure variable that **prodptr** points to.

MISCELLANEOUS

?:

- *Usage*: *ae ? e1 : e2*
  or
  pe ? e1 : e2
  If *ae* or *pe* is true then *e1* is evaluated; otherwise *e2* is evaluated. The value is *e1* or *e2*.
- *Example*: abs = (i <= 0) ? i : −i;

,

- *Usage*: *e1 , e2*
  First evaluate *e1*, then *e2*. Value of the expression is *e2*.
- *Example*: for (i = A, j = B;
      i < j;
      i++, j−−)
     p[i] = p[j];

sizeof

- *Usage*: *sizeof(e)*
  Number of bytes required by the type of *e*. If *e* is an array expression, then *e* refers to the entire array, *not* to the address of the first elements, as in other contexts.

- *Usage*: *sizeof(type)*
  Number of bytes occupied by an object of type *type*.
- *Example*: n = sizeof(arname) / sizeof(int);
  The number of elements in an *int* array is given by the number of bytes in the array, divided by the number of bytes in each element.

(type)

- *Usage*: *(type)e*
  Value of *e* converted to type *type*.
- *Example*: x = (float)n / 3;
  The *int* value of *n* is converted to *float* before dividing by *3*.

()

- *Usage*: *fe(e1, e2, ...eN)*
  Call function *fe* with arguments e1, e2, ...eN. The value of the expression is the value returned by the function. Note that the order of evaluation of *e1* through *eN* is *not* guaranteed.
  Note — See **FUNCTIONS** on page 26.
- *Example*: x = sqrt(y);

PRECEDENCE AND ASSOCIATIVITY

- **PRECEDENCE** — In the chart below, the operators within a group have equal precedence. *Higher precedence operator groups are higher in the chart*.
- **ASSOCIATIVITY** — In the absence of explicit parentheses, associativity rules are used to determine how to group operators and operands (*left-to-right*, or *right-to-left*), when the operators are in the same group.
  - *Examples —*
    - *a * b / c* is equivalent to *(a * b) / c* because of *left-to-right* associativity.
    - *a = b = c* is equivalent to *a = (b = c)* because of *right-to-left* associativity.

()	Function call (page 17)	LEFT-TO-RIGHT
[]	Array element (page 16)	
.	Structure or union member (page 16)	
−>	Structure or union member using pointer (page 16)	
!	Logical not (page 14)	*RIGHT-TO-LEFT*
~	One's complement (page 15)	
−	Minus (page 10)	
++	Increment (page 11)	
−−	Decrement (page 11)	
&	Address (page 16)	
*	Indirection (page 16)	
(type)	Type cast (page 17)	
sizeof	Size in bytes (page 17)	
*	Multiply (page 10)	LEFT-TO-RIGHT
/	Divide (page 10)	
%	Remainder (page 10)	
+	Add (page 10)	LEFT-TO-RIGHT
−	Subtract (page 10)	
<<	Left shift (page 15)	LEFT-TO-RIGHT
>>	Right shift (page 15)	
<	Less than (page 13)	LEFT-TO-RIGHT
<=	Less than or equal (page 14)	
>	Greater than (page 14)	
>=	Greater than or equal (page 14)	
==	Equal (page 13)	LEFT-TO-RIGHT
!=	Not equal (page 13)	
&	Bitwise and (page 15)	LEFT-TO-RIGHT
^	Bitwise exclusive or (page 15)	LEFT-TO-RIGHT
|	Bitwise or (page 15)	LEFT-TO-RIGHT
&&	Logical and (page 14)	LEFT-TO-RIGHT
||	Logical or (page 14)	LEFT-TO-RIGHT
?:	Conditional (page 17)	*RIGHT-TO-LEFT*
=	Assignment (pages 12-13)	*RIGHT-TO-LEFT*
*= /= %= += −= <<= >>= &= ^= |=		
,	Comma (page 17)	LEFT-TO-RIGHT

OPERAND EVALUATION ORDER

- Four operators — **&&** || **?:** **,** — guarantee that the *left*most operand will always be evaluated *first*. For other operators, the order of evaluation may vary among compilers. This means that even though you test a program on one computer, if the code depends on *un*guaranteed order of evaluation, the program may fail if it is compiled and run on other computers.

- *Example* —
  v = (x = 5) + (++x);
  If the order of evaluation of the + operands is *left-to-right*, the value of *v* would be *11 (5 + 6)*, and the value of *x* would be *6*. If the order is *right-to-left*, the value of *v* depends on the value of *x* before the expression is evaluated; for instance, if *x* was *0*, the value of *v* would be *6 (5 + 1)*, and the value of *x* would be *5*.

- *Caution* — When you make an assignment to a variable in *any* kind of expression (including function calls), do *not* use that variable again in the same expression. For instance, in the above example, if you want left-to-right evaluation, use:
  x = 5;
  v = x + (x + 1);
  ++x;

ARITHMETIC CONVERSIONS

- First, any operands of type *char* or *short* are converted to *int*, and any operands of type *unsigned char* or *unsigned short* are converted to *unsigned int*.

- Then, if either operand is *double*, the other is converted to *double* and that is the type of the result.

- Otherwise, if either operand is *unsigned long*, the other is converted to *unsigned long* and that is the type of the result.

- Otherwise, if either operand is *long*, the other is converted to *long* and that is the type of the result.

- Otherwise, if one operand is *long*, and the other is *unsigned int*, they are both converted to *unsigned long* and that is the type of the result.

- Otherwise, if either operand is *unsigned*, the other is converted to *unsigned* and that is the type of the result.

- Otherwise, both operands must be *int*, and that is the type of the result.

STATEMENTS

FORMAT AND NESTING

- *Format* —
  - A single statement may be on one or more lines.
  - Two or more statements may be on one line.

- *Nesting* — Control flow statements (*if, if-else, switch, while, do-while*, and *for*) can be nested.

STATEMENT LABEL

- May precede any statement. Purpose is to be the target of a *goto* statement.

- Consists of identifier followed by colon (*:*).

- Scope of label is current function.

- *Example* — ABC2: x = 3;

COMPOUND STATEMENT (BLOCK)

- A compound statement is composed of one or more statements of any type shown below.

- The entire compound statement is enclosed in braces ({ }).

- *No* semicolon (*;*) after terminating brace (}).

- *Example* — {x = 1; y = 2; z = 3;}

EXPRESSION STATEMENTS

Note — Any expression, when terminated with a semicolon (*;*), becomes a statement. The following are examples of expression statements.

- *Assignment Statement*
  - identifier = expression;
  - *Example* — x = 3;

- *Function Call Statement*
  - funcname (arg1, ..., argN);
  - *Example* — fclose (file);

- *Null Statement*
  - Consists of *only* a semicolon (*;*).
  - Useful as null body of control flow statement.

break;

- Terminates smallest enclosing *switch*, *while, do*, or *for* statement. Passes control to the statement following the terminated statement. One use of *break* is to leave a loop when a specified value of a variable is found.

- *Example* — for (i=0; i<n; i++)
                if ((a[i] = b[i]) == 0)
                    break;

continue;

- Goes to top of smallest enclosing *while, do*, or *for* statement, causing it to repeat execution. This is the *opposite* of the *break* statement.

- *Example* — for (i=0; i<n; i++) {
                if (a[i] != 0)
                    continue;
                a[i] = b[i];
                k++;
            }

return;

- Exits a function.

return expression;

- Exits a function and returns the value of an expression.

- *Example* — return x+y;

goto label;

- Goes unconditionally to statement with *label*.

- Useful to break out of nested control flow statements.

- Scope is limited to current function.

- *Example* — goto ABC;

if (expression)
statement

- If expression is —
  - *True* — Statement is executed.
  - *False* — Nothing is executed.

- *Example* — if (a == x)
  ```
                temp = 3;
            temp = 5;
  ```

if (expression)
statement1
else
statement2

- If expression is —
  - *True* — Statement1 is executed, and control passes to the statement *following* statement2 (that is, statement2 is *not* executed).
  - *False* — Statement2 is executed.

- The *else* part of the statement is optional. Therefore, ambiguity exists when the *else* is omitted from a nested *if* sequence. In such cases, the *else* is associated with the closest previous un-*else*'ed *if* at the same block level.

- *Examples* —
  - *else* associated with second *if*:
    ```
    if (x > 1)
       if (y==2)
          z=5;
       else
          z=6;
    ```
  - *else* associated with first *if*:
    ```
    if (x> 1) {
       if (y==2)
          z=5;
    } else
          z=6;
    ```
  - Nested *if*'s —
    ```
    if (x == 'a')
       y = 1;
    else if (x == 'b') {
       y = 2;
       z = 3;
    } else if (x == 'c')
       y = 4;
    else
       printf("ERROR");
    ```

switch (expression) {

   case constant: statements

   case constant: statements

   ...

   default: statements

}

- Compares expression to constants in all *case* statements, and branches to the statement that matches the expression.

- Each *case* must be labeled by either an integer or a character constant or constant expression. A constant expression cannot involve variables or function calls.
  - *Examples* —
    - case 3+4: Correct.
    - case X+Y: Incorrect.

- The *default* case is executed if no match is obtained on any other *case*.
  - The *default* need *not* be the last case.
  - If *default* is not included and no match occurs, no action takes place.

- The *cases* serve merely as labels and once the code for a *case* is executed, control falls through to the next *case* unless a *break* statement is included. This allows a single action for multiple cases.

- No two *case* constants within the same switch may have the same value.

- *Example*
  ```
  switch (x) {
    case 'A':
      printf("CASE A\n");
      break;
    case 'B':
    case 'C':
      printf("CASE B or C\n");
      break;
    default:
      printf("NOT A,B, or C\n");
      break;
  }
  ```

- The most general syntactic form of the *switch* statement is as follows —

        switch (expression) statement
  - *Example* —
    ```
    switch (x)
    case 2:
    case 4:
      y = 3;
    ```

while (expression)
statement

- If expression is —
    - **True** — Statement is executed until expression becomes false.
    - **False** — Execution resumes at the following statement.
    - **Note** — The expression is evaluated **before** the statement is executed. Therefore, if the expression is false the first time through, the statement is never executed.

- **Example** — while (k < n) {
                    y = y * x;
                    k++;
                }

do
statement
while (expression);

- Statement is executed. If expression is —
    - **True** — Statement is executed and expression is evaluated ... this is repeated until statement becomes false.
    - **False** — Execution resumes at following statement.

- **Note** — The expression is evaluated **after** the statement is executed. Thus the statement is executed at least once.
  do-while tests loop at **bottom**.
  while tests loop at **top**.

- **Example** — x = 1;
                do
                    printf("%d\n", power(x, 2));
                while (++x <= 7);

for (expression1;
expression2;
expression3)
statement

- *expression* —
  - *1* — Loop initialization.
  - *2* — Test made *before* each iteration. If:
    - *True* —
      - Execute *statement* following *for*.
      - Execute *expression3*.
      - Iterate until *expression2* is false.
    - *False* — Exit loop by transferring control to statement following *for* statement.
  - *3* — Evaluated after each iteration.

- The *for* statement is equivalent to —
  ```
  expression1;
  while (expression2) {
     statement
     expression3;
  }
  ```

- *Example* — for (x = 1; x <= 7; x++)
  ```
                printf("%d\n", power(x, 2));
  ```

- Any or all of the three *for* expressions may be omitted; however, the semicolons (*;*) must remain.
  - If *expression2* is omitted, it is taken as permanently true.
  - *for (;;)* is an infinite loop, equivalent to *while(1)*.

- The comma (*,*) operator can be used to put multiple expressions within parts of the *for* statement.
  - *Example* — for (i=0, j=n−1; i < n; i++, j−−)
    ```
                  a[i] = a[j];
    ```

FUNCTIONS

FUNCTION DEFINITION

- A function is defined by declaring its parameters and type of value returned (if any), and writing a compound statement (or block) that specifies what the function does.
  - *Example —*

```
          ─type
            ─function name
              ─parameter list
    double
    linfunc (x, a, b)
    double x; ⎫
    double a; ⎬ declaration of
    double b; ⎭ parameters
    {            returned value   ⎫
          return (a*x + b);       ⎬ compound
    }                             ⎭ statement
```

- The *return* statement in a function can return no value, or the value of the expression in the *return* statement. If required, the expression is converted to the type of the function in which it appears.

- A function that does not return anything should be declared as type *void*.
  - *Example —*
    ```
    void
    errmesg(s)
    char *s;
    {
        printf("***%s\n", s);
    }
    ```

FUNCTION CALL

- Two common ways to call a function —
  - funcname (e1, e2, ..., eN)
  - (*funcptr) (e1, e2, ..., eN)

  A function pointer, *funcptr*, is a variable that contains the address of a function. The address of a function named *funcname* can be assigned to *funcptr* by the statement

  funcptr = funcname;

- Arguments are passed by value. That is, each expression is evaluated and the value is passed to the function, for instance, by loading the values on a stack.

- The order in which the argument expressions are evaluated is *not* guaranteed, nor is the order in which values are loaded on a stack.

- There is *no* run-time check on the number or the types of arguments passed to a function. You can use the *UNIX* system *lint* command to perform such checks before the program is compiled. (See *lint* on page 64.)

- The value of a function call as an expression is the value returned by the function.

- The declared type of a function should match the type of the value returned. For example, if the *linfunc* function returns a *double*, then the function should be declared as *double* where it is called, using the declaration —

  extern double linfunc();

  Note — Such declarations do *not* define a function, but merely declare the type of value returned, and generally are not necessary in the file where the function is defined.
  (See *DECLARATIONS* on page 29.)

- *Examples* —
  - *Correct* — extern double linfunc();

    float y;

    y = linfunc (3.05, 4.0, 1e−3);

    The value of the function call is properly converted from *double* to *float* by the assignment to *y*.
  - *Incorrect* —float x;

    float y;

    x = 3.05;

    y = linfunc (x, 4, 1e−3);

    This is wrong because types of arguments do not match declarations in definition, that is —

    4 is *int*, not *double*

    The result is that arguments passed on the stack are the wrong size and format, so that arguments taken off the stack by the *linfunc* function are nonsense. There is no predictable return value. Also, unless the type of *linfunc* is declared, it is presumed to be type *int*. Thus even if the *linfunc* function did return a meaningful *double*, the value of the function call expression would be a nonsensical *int* value (e.g., upper half of a *double*).

main FUNCTION

- The start of every program is a *main()* function.

- When a program is executed, arguments to the program are made available to *main()* through the *argc* and *argv* parameters.

- Shell environment variables are made available through the *env* parameter.

- *Example* —

```
/*
 * program that prints arguments
 * followed by environment
 */
main (argc, argv, envp)
int argc;        /* number of arguments */
char **argv; /* string arguments vector */
char **envp; /* environment variables vector */
{
    register int i;
    register char **p;

    /* print arguments */
    for (i=0; i<argc; i++)
        printf("arg %i:%s\n", i, argv[i]);
    /* print environment */
    for (p=envp; *p != (char*)0; p++)
        printf ("%s\n", *p);
}
```

- *Note* — The *argv* and *envp* parameters could also be declared by —
```
    char *argv[];
    char *envp[];
```

DECLARATIONS

INTRODUCTION

Declarations are used to define variables, and to declare the types of variables and functions defined elsewhere. Declarations are also used to define new data types in terms of existing types.

A declaration is *not* a statement.

BASIC TYPES

- *Examples —*
  - char c;
  - int x;

- The basic types are —

char	Character (one byte)
int	Integer (usually one word)
unsigned	Non-negative integer (same size as integer)
short	Small integer (word or halfword)
long	Large integer (word or doubleword)
float	Floating point (single precision)
double	Floating point (double precision)
void	No value (typically to discard the value of a function call)

- *char* may be signed or unsigned depending on the compiler. Used as an integer, a signed *char* has values from −127 to 128, while an unsigned *char* has values from 0 to 256.

- Some implementations support an explicit *unsigned char*.

- *int* may be the same as either *long* or *short*.

- *unsigned* by itself is equivalent to *unsigned int*.

- *unsigned* can modify *char*, *short*, or *long* — *unsigned char*, *unsigned short*, *unsigned long*.

- *short* and *long* are equivalent to *short int* or *long int*, respectively.

- *long* is typically twice the size of *short*.

POINTERS AND ARRAYS

Note — There are an infinite number of pointer and array data types. The following are common examples.

- *Pointer to a basic type.*
  - *Example* — char *p;
    p is a pointer to a character, that is, *p* should be assigned the address of a character variable.

- *Pointer to a pointer.*
  - *Example* — char **t;
    t is a pointer to a character pointer.

- *One-dimensional array.*
  - *Example* — int a[50];
    a is an array of 50 integers.

- *Two-dimensional array.*
  - *Example* — char m[7][50];
    m is an array of 7 arrays of 50 characters each.

- *Array of 7 pointers.*
  - *Example* — char *r[7];
    r is an array of pointers to characters.

- *Pointer to a function.*
  - *Example* — int (*f)();
    f is a pointer to a function that returns an integer value.

STRUCTURES — struct

- A structure is a conglomerate data type comprising several other member data types, typically related to each other in some logical way.

- **Defining a structure data type.**
  A structure data type is defined by a declaration that is of the form —
  ```
  struct struct_name {
          member_declarations
      };
  ```
  - **Example —**
  ```
  struct dinner {
          char        *place;
          float       cost;
          struct dinner *next;
      };
  ```

- **Declaring a structure variable.**
  Once a structure data type has been defined, variables can be declared.
  - **Examples —**
    - struct dinner week_days [7];
      Array of structures.
    - struct dinner best_one;
      Single structure variable.
    - struct dinner *p;
      Pointer to structure variable.

BIT FIELDS IN STRUCTURES — struct

- A bit field is a structure member defined as a number of bits, usually less than the number of bits in an integer. The idea behind fields is to match externally imposed storage layouts, or to save storage space.

- **Example —**
  ```
  struct bfeg {
              unsigned int bf_fld1 : 10;
              unsigned int bf_fld2 : 6;
      };
  ```
  Structure comprises a 10-bit field that is converted to type *unsigned int* when used in an expression, and a 6-bit field that is converted to *unsigned int*.

UNIONS — union

- A union is a variable that can be any one of a set of members.

- *Defining a union data type.*
  A union data type is defined by a declaration similar to that of a structure.
      union union_name {
          member_declarations
      };
  - *Example —*
    union bigword {
            long bg_long;
            char *bg_char[4];
    };
    The new type, *union bigword*, is as large as the largest of the members, and is aligned to an address suitable for both *long* and *char*[4].

- *Declaring a union variable.*
  - *Examples —*
    - union bigword x;
    - union bigword *p;
    - union bigword a[100];

ENUMERATIONS — enum

- An enumeration type has values limited to one of a specified set.

- *Defining an enum data type.*
  enum enum_name {
          list_of_values
  };

  - Each value that the specified type of enumeration can take is an identifier.
  - *Example —*
    enum color {
            red, green, yellow
    };

- *Declaring an enum variable.*
  - *Examples —*
    - enum color chair;
    - enum color suite [40];

- *Using an enum variable in an expression.*
  - *Examples —*
    - chair = red
    - suite[5] != yellow

RENAMING A TYPE — typedef

- **Format** —
  typedef existing_type new_type

- **Examples** —
  - typedef long large;
    Defines type large equivalent to **long**.
  - typedef char *string;
    Defines type string equivalent to **char ***.

- May be used —
  - As a mnemonic or abbreviation (more readable programs).
  - To facilitate portability (the **typedef** for the data type may differ across machines).

DEFINING A VARIABLE — WITHIN A BLOCK

Note 1 — **Permanent variables**, that is, variables stored in the data area, are initialized to 0's unless otherwise specified in the declaration. **Temporary variables**, that is, variables stored on a stack or in a register, are not initialized unless specified in the declaration.

Note 2 — Within a block, all declarations must precede the first statement.

Automatic

- **Example** —
  ```
  {
          int x;
          ...
  }
  ```
  x is an **automatic** variable.

- Temporary. Lost when the block is completed.

- Scope is the block in which the variable is defined.

- Any block variable declaration takes precedence over more global definition.

Register

- *Example* —
  ```
  {
          register int y;
          ...
  }
  ```

- Temporary. Stored in machine register if possible.

- Register variables can be accessed more quickly.

- Any block variable with data size no larger than a machine register can be stored in a register.

- If there are not enough registers, then the variables are stored as automatic.

- Scope is the block.

- The address operator, **&**, *cannot* be applied to register variables.

Formal Parameter

- *Examples* —
  - ```
    int func(x)
    int x;
    {
        ...
    }
    ```
  - ```
    int func(x)
    register int x;
    {
        ...
    }
    ```

- Temporary.

- Initialized to values of arguments passed to function.

- Scope is the function block.

- Should have names distinct from external level variables or block variables defined within the function.

- Values can be assigned to formal parameters within the function block.

Static

- *Example* —
  ```
  {
      static int flag;
      ...
  }
  ```

- Permanent. Value is not lost when function returns.

- Any block variable, except function formal parameters, can be defined as *static*.

- Scope is the block.

DEFINING A VARIABLE — EXTERNAL LEVEL

Global

- *Example —*
  int Global_flag;

- Defined at the same level as functions, that is, not inside a block.

- Permanent.

- Initialized to 0's unless otherwise specified.

- Scope is the entire program.

- Must be declared in every file where used. *Note —* Some compilers require that a global variable can be defined in exactly one file, and must be declared as *extern* where used in other files. (See *DECLARING OBJECTS DEFINED ELSEWHERE* on page 38.)

- Should be declared before first use in file.

Static

- *Example —*
  static int File_flag;

- Permanent.

- Scope is file in which the variable is defined.

- Should be declared before first use in file.

INITIALIZATION

- Any variable except a formal parameter or an automatic array, structure, or union, can be initialized when defined.

- Any permanent variable is initialized to 0 (NULL) unless otherwise specified.

- Any constant expression can be used as an initialization value.

Basic Types

- *Examples* —
  - int i = 1;
  - float x = 3.145e−2;

Arrays

- *Examples* —
  - int a[] = {1, 4, 9, 16, 25, 36};
  - char s[20] = {'a', 'b', 'c'};

- List of array values must be enclosed by braces.

- If array dimension given, then values not explicitly listed are 0.

- If array dimension omitted, then array size is the same as the number of values.

Strings

- *Example* —
  char s[] = "hello";

  Equivalent to
  char s[] = {'h', 'e', 'l', 'l', 'o', '\0'};

Structures

- *Example* —
  ```
  struct person {
          int   height;
          char gender;
  };
  struct person x = {70, 'Y'};
  struct person family[] = {
          {73, 'X'},
          {68, 'Y'},
          {50, 'X'}
  };
  ```

- List of values for each structure variable should be enclosed in braces, although if the number of values matches the number of structure members this is not necessary.

- Values assigned to members in same order as structure definition.

- Value list can be incomplete, in which case the remaining values are 0.

  - *Example* —
    ```
    struct person people [10] = {
            {68},
            {71},
            {74}
    };
    ```
    The *height* members of the first three structure variables in the array are explicitly initialized; other members are initialized to 0.

DECLARING OBJECTS DEFINED ELSEWHERE — *extern*

- The types of external level objects (i.e., variables and functions) defined elsewhere should be declared. Failure to make such declarations may result in a compiler or loader error or code that does not work properly.

- Prepend the keyword ***extern*** to the declaration that would be used to define the object.
  - *Examples* —
    - extern int Global_var;
    - extern char *Name;
    - extern int func();

- Omit the dimension of a one-dimensional array, if you wish.
  - *Example* —
    extern float Num_array[];

- Since all functions are defined on the external level, for declarations of functions within a block ***extern*** is redundant and is often omitted.
  - *Example* —
    ```
    {
          ...
        int func();
          ...
    }
    ```

- A function that is defined as type ***void*** should be declared as ***void***. In the absence of an explicit declaration, a function is taken to be type ***int***.

- At the external level, the scope of a declaration is the remainder of the file; within a block, the scope is the block. Normally external level ***extern*** declarations are placed at the head of a file.

- For some compilers, ***extern*** may be omitted from the declaration for variables declared at the external level. Multiple definitions of external level variables are resolved by the loader.

PREPROCESSOR

INTRODUCTION

A **#** as the first character on a line designates a preprocessor control line. Control lines are terminated by a Newline. Use a Backslash (\) just before the Newline to continue a control line.

TOKEN REPLACEMENT

#define identifier string
- **Example** — #define ABC 100
  Substitutes 100 for every occurrence of **ABC** as a token.

#undef identifier
- **Example** — #undef ABC
  Cancels previous **#define** for identifier **ABC**, if any.

MACROS

Note — To avoid expression errors, enclose a macro parameter in parentheses everywhere it occurs in a macro definition.

#define identifier1(identifier2,...) string
- **Example** — #define abs(A) (((A) > 0) ? (A) : −(A))
  Substitutes **((arg) > 0) ? (arg) : −(arg)** for **abs(arg)**, replacing each occurrence of **A** by **arg**.
- **Example** — #define nmem (P, N)\
          (P) → p_mem [N].u_long
  The \ is used to continue the macro definition across two lines. This macro hides the complexity of an expression involving an array of unions within a structure.

FILE INCLUSION

Note — **#include** control lines may appear anywhere, but most are placed near the beginning of a file.

#include <filename>
- **Example** — #include <math.h>
  Replaces this line with contents of file **math.h**. The angle brackets specify that **math.h** should be found in a "standard" directory, such as **/usr/include**. Does **not** search directory of the source file.

#include "filename"
- **Example** — #include "ABC"
  Replaces this line with contents of file **ABC**. With "**ABC**" instead of <**ABC**>, **ABC** is sought in the directory of the source file being processed. If not found there, then it is sought along the search path specified by the −**I** option to the preprocessor. If it is not found along that path, "standard" directories are searched.

CONDITIONAL COMPILATION

Conditional compilation control lines are used to compile different code depending on externally defined conditions.

#if constant-expression
- **Example** — #if ABC + 3
  True if **ABC**+3 evaluates to non-zero.

#ifdef identifier
- **Example** — #ifdef ABC
  True if **ABC is** currently defined by **#define**.

#ifndef identifier
- **Example** — #ifndef ABC
  True if **ABC** is **not** currently defined by **#define**.

#else
...
#endif
- If preceding **#if, #ifdef**, or **#ifndef** test is —
  - **True** — Lines between **#else** and **#endif** are ignored.
  - **False** — Lines between the test and a **#else** or, lacking a **#else**, the **#endif**, are ignored.
- **#endif** terminates the conditional compilation.

- **Example** —
  ```
  #ifdef DEBUG
  fprintf (stderr, "location: x = %d\n", x);
  #endif
  ```

LINE NUMBER AND FILE NAME

#line constant "filename"
- **Example** — #line 20 "ABC"
  Changes line number and filename. The filename may be omitted.

PROGRAM STRUCTURE

INTRODUCTION

The example program on the following pages reads up to
MAXLINES lines from standard input, sorts the lines in either
increasing or decreasing order depending on a flag passed as an
argv argument to **main()**, and writes the sorted lines to standard
output. Standard I/O (i.e., **stdin** and **stdout**) may be
a terminal, a pipe, or a file.

bblsort.h

A
```
#define MAXLINES    100
#define LINESIZE    (132 + 1)
```

main.c

B
```
#include <stdio.h>
#include "bblsort.h"
```

C
```
char Line[MAXLINES][LINESIZE];  /* line buffer */
int  Revflg;                    /* reverse flag */
```

```
/*
 * sort text lines in lexicographic order
 */
```
D
```
main(argc, argv)
char **argv; /* command line arguments */
int   argc;    /* number of arguments */
{
```
E
```
    int  rdlines();
    void bblsort(), wrlines();
```
F
```
    int  numlines;
```
G
```
    Revflg = (argc > 1 && argv[1][0] == '-');
    numlines = rdlines();
    bblsort(numlines);
    wrlines(numlines);
}
```

```
/*
 * read lines from standard input
 */
```
H
```
static int
rdlines()
{
    char      *fgets();
```
I
```
    register int  i;
```
```
    for (i = 0; i < MAXLINES; i++)
        if (fgets(Line[i], LINESIZE, stdin)
```
J
```
                == (char *)NULL)
            break;
    return (i);
}
```

```
/*
 * write lines to standard output
 */
```
K
```
static void
wrlines(n)
```
L
```
register int  n; /* number of lines */
{
    register int  i;

    for (i = 0; i < n; i++)
        fputs(Line[i], stdout);
}
```

EXPLANATION

A   Parameters that apply across a program are usually placed in a separate file that can be included in other files as needed. If the parameters need to be changed, only this one file is affected.

B   Included files are usually placed at the beginning of a file. The *stdio.h* include file defines the *stdin*, *stdout*, and *NULL* expressions used in conjunction with the *fgets()* and *fputs()* functions.

C   External variable declarations are usually placed near the beginning of a file. Here, a global array of line buffers and a global reverse order flag are defined.

D   The *main()* function formal parameters should be declared if used. *main()* is the start of the program.

E   The types of functions called in a function block should normally be declared.

F   *numlines* is declared to be an automatic integer variable for use within the block.

G   By convention the first *argv* argument passed to *main()* is the name of the program. *argv[1]* is the second argument, and *argv[1][0]* the first character of the second argument. Note that *argc* is checked before the expression *argv[1][0]* is evaluated, since if there is no second argument, the *argv[1][0]* expression does not make sense.

H   The *rdlines()* function returns the number of lines read, represented as an integer, hence *rdlines()* is defined to be of type *int*. *static* specifies that the function is used only within this file.

I   *i* is defined for block use. The *register* declaration is an attempt to improve the efficiency of the following *for* loop.

J   Since *fgets()* is of type *char **, the value returned by *fgets()* should be compared to a NULL *character pointer*, hence the *(char *)* type cast.

K   The *wrlines()* function does not return a value, and is therefore declared as type *void*.

L   The formal parameter, *n*, is declared to be *register* for efficiency.

bblsort.c

M
```
# include "bblsort.h"
```

N
```
extern char  Line[][LINESIZE];
```

```
    /*
     * bubble sort
     */
```
O
```
void
bblsort(n)
register int  n;  /* number of lines */
{
    int           lexcmp();
    void          swap();
    register int  i, j;

    for (i = 1; i <= n - 1; i++)
        for (j = n - 1; j >= i; j--)
            if (lexcmp(j - 1, j))
                swap(j - 1, j);
}
```

```
    /*
     * lexicographic comparison of two lines
     */
    static int
    lexcmp(i, j)
```
P
```
register int  i, j;  /* line array elements */
{
```
Q
```
    int           strcmp();
    extern int    Revflg;
    register int  lc;

    lc = strcmp(Line[i], Line[j]);
```
R
```
    return ((lc < 0 && Revflg)
            || (lc > 0 && !Revflg));
}
```

```
    /*
     * swap lines
     */
    static void
    swap(i, j)
    register int  i, j;  /* line array elements */
    {
        char  *strcpy();
        char  temp[LINESIZE];

        strcpy(temp, Line[i]);
        strcpy(Line[i], Line[j]);
        strcpy(Line[j], temp);
    }
```

EXPLANATION

M **bblsort.h** is included to define **LINESIZE**.

N This declaration of **Line** applies to the entire file; the type of **Line** is **declared**, but **Line** is not **defined** here.

O **bblsort()** is not declared **static** because it is called by **main()** which is defined in another file.

P Both **i** and **j** are defined in the same declaration. The order of **i** and **j** in this declaration is immaterial.

Q The global flag **Revflg** must be declared **extern**, indicating that **Revflg** is defined elsewhere. **Revflg** could also be declared with **Line** near the beginning of the file.

R The value of the expression is either true (1) or false (0) which are integer values. Hence **lexcmp()** is declared to be of type **int**.

I/O LIBRARY

INTRODUCTION

The name of the manual page in the *UNIX System V Programmer Reference Manual* is shown for each function listed here. These and other functions are completely specified in *Section 3* of the *Manual*.

stdio.h should be included whenever functions in this section are used. The appropriate preprocessor control line is —
#include <stdio.h>
* *stdio.h* defines *FILE* data type.
* Defines parameters used in library function calls and macros.
  * *Examples* —
    * *stdin* — Standard input
    * *stdout* — Standard output
    * *stderr* — Error output
    * *NULL* — Null (0) pointer
    * *EOF* — End-of-file
  * *Note* — *stdin*, *stdout* and *stderr* refer to the terminal, unless redirected to or from a file or a pipe.
* Defines the following macros —
  putc()   ferror()
  getc()   clearerr()
  putchar()   feof()
  getchar()   fileno()

Note — An I/O *stream* is identified by a *FILE* pointer. Buffers are associated with a stream as part of the standard I/O package.

FILE ACCESS

- *fopen* — Open an I/O stream.
  - Manual Page: fopen(3S)
  - Synopsis: FILE *fopen (filename, type)
        char *filename, *type;

- *freopen* — Close stream and open named file using some stream identification.
  - Manual Page: fopen(3S)
  - Synopsis: FILE *freopen (newfile, type, stream)
        char *newfile, *type;
        FILE *stream;

- *fdopen* — Associate stream with an **open(2)** file descriptor.
  - Manual Page: fopen(3S)
  - Synopsis: FILE *fdopen (fildes, type)
        int fildes;
        char *type;

- *fclose* — Close an open I/O stream.
  - Manual Page: fclose(3S)
  - Synopsis: int fclose (stream)
        FILE *stream;

- *fflush* — Write all currently buffered characters in output stream.
  - Manual Page: fclose(3S)
  - Synopsis: int fflush (stream)
        FILE *stream;

- *fseek* — Reposition stream pointer.
  - Manual Page: fseek(3S)
  - Synopsis: int fseek (stream, offset, ptrname)
        FILE *stream;
        long offset;
        int ptrname;

- *ftell* — Return current file offset.
  - Manual Page: fseek(3S)
  - Synopsis: long ftell (stream)
        FILE *stream;

- *rewind* — Reposition stream pointer at beginning of file.
  - Manual Page: fseek(3S)
  - Synopsis: void rewind (stream)
        FILE *stream;

- *setbuf* — Modify stream buffering.
  - Manual Page: setbuf(3S)
  - Synopsis: void setbuf (stream, buf)
            FILE *stream;
            char *buf;

- *setvbuf* — Modify stream buffering.
  - Manual Page: setbuf(3S)
  - Synopsis: int setvbuf (stream, buf, type, size)
            FILE *stream;
            char *buf;
            int type, size;

PIPE ACCESS

- *pclose* — Close a stream opened by *popen*.
  - Manual Page: popen(3S)
  - Synopsis: int pclose (stream)
            FILE *stream;

- *popen* — Create pipe as an inter-process stream.
  - Manual Page: popen(3S)
  - Synopsis: FILE *popen (command, type)
            char *command, *type;

FILE STATUS

- *clearerr* — Reset error condition on stream.
  - Manual Page: ferror(3S)
  - Synopsis: void clearerr (stream)
            FILE *stream;

- *feof* — Test for end-of-file on stream.
  - Manual Page: ferror(3S)
  - Synopsis: int feof (stream)
            FILE *stream;

- *ferror* — Test for error condition on stream.
  - Manual Page: ferror(3S)
  - Synopsis: int ferror (stream)
            FILE *stream;

- *fileno* — *open(2)* file descriptor associated with an open stream.
  - Manual Page: ferror(3S)
  - Synopsis: int fileno (stream)
            FILE *stream;

FORMATTED I/O

- For *printf, fprintf,* and *sprintf,*
  see *FORMATTED OUTPUT* on page 56.

- For *scanf, fscanf,* and *sscanf,*
  see *FORMATTED INPUT* on page 60.

STRING I/O

- *fgets* — Read line from stream. Newline is included.
  - Manual Page: gets(3S)
  - Synopsis: char *fgets (s, n, stream)
    - char *s;
    - int n;
    - FILE *stream;

- *gets* — Read line from standard input (i.e., **stdin**). Newline is discarded.
  - Manual Page: gets(3S)
  - Synopsis: char *gets (s)
    - char *s;

- *fputs* — Write string to stream.
  - Manual Page: puts(3S)
  - Synopsis: int fputs (s, stream)
    - char *s;
    - FILE *stream;

- *puts* — Write string to standard output (i.e., **stdout**). Newline character is appended.
  - Manual Page: puts(3S)
  - Synopsis: int puts (s)
    - char *s;

SINGLE CHARACTER I/O — INPUT

- *fgetc* — Read next character from stream.
  - Manual Page: getc(3S)
  - Synopsis: int fgetc (stream)
    - FILE *stream;

Note — **getc()**, **getchar()** and **ungetc()** are defined as macros.

- *getc* — Read next character from stream.
  - Manual Page: getc(3S)
  - Synopsis: int getc (stream)
    - FILE *stream;

- *getchar* — Read next character from **stdin**.
  - Manual Page: getc(3S)
  - Synopsis: int getchar ()

- *ungetc* — Replace last character read from stream.
  - Manual Page: ungetc(3S)
  - Synopsis: int ungetc (c, stream)
    - int c;
    - FILE *stream;

SINGLE CHARACTER I/O — OUTPUT

Manual Page — All of the functions in this section
are on the ***putc(3S)*** manual page.

- *fputc* — Write character to stream.
  - Synopsis: int fputc (c, stream)
                int c;
                FILE *stream;

Note — ***putc()*** and ***putchar()*** are defined as macros.

- *putc* — Write character to stream.
  - Synopsis: int putc (c, stream)
                int c;
                FILE *stream;

- *putchar* — Write character to **stdout**.
  - Synopsis: int putchar (c)
                int c;

BLOCK I/O

Manual Page — The functions in this section are on the
fread(3S) manual page.

- *fread* — Read specified number of bytes (characters)
  from stream.
  - Synopsis: int fread (ptr, size, nitems, stream)
                char *ptr;
                int size, nitems;
                FILE *stream;

- *fwrite* — Write specified number of bytes to stream.
  - Synopsis: int fwrite (ptr, size, nitems, stream)
                char *ptr;
                int size, nitems;
                FILE *stream;

OTHER LIBRARIES

INTRODUCTION

Some commonly used library functions are listed here.
This is *not* a complete list.

The name of the manual page in the *UNIX System V Programmer Reference Manual* is shown for each function.

EXECUTING ANOTHER PROGRAM

Note — To use this function,
#include <stdio.h>

- *system* — Execute shell command.
  - Manual Page: system(3S)
  - Synopsis: int system (string)
            char *string;

TEMPORARY FILES

Note — To use functions in this section,
#include <stdio.h>

- *tmpnam* — Create temporary filename.
  - Manual Page: tmpnam(3S)
  - Synopsis: char *tmpnam (s)
            char *s;

- *tempnam* — Create temporary filename using specified directory and file prefix.
  - Manual Page: tmpnam(3S)
  - Synopsis: char *tempnam (dir, pfx)
            char *dir, *pfx;

- *mktemp* — Create a unique filename using a template.
  - Manual Page: mktemp(3C)
  - Synopsis: char *mktemp (template)
            char *template;

- *tmpfile* — Create temporary file.
  - Manual Page: tmpfile(3S)
  - Synopsis: FILE *tmpfile ()

STRING MANIPULATION

Manual Page — All of the functions in this section are on the **string(3C)** manual page.

Note — The file **string.h** contains **extern** declarations for the functions in this section. This file may be included by —
        #include <string.h>

- *strcat* — Concatenate two strings.
  - Synopsis: char *strcat (s1, s2)
            char *s1, *s2;

- *strncat* — Concatenate two strings. At most *n* characters are appended.
  - Synopsis: char *strncat (s1, s2, n)
            char *s1, *s2;
            int n;

- *strcmp* — Lexicographically compare two strings.
  - Synopsis: int strcmp (s1, s2)
            char *s1, *s2;

- *strncmp* — Compare first *n* characters of two strings.
  - Synopsis: int strncmp (s1, s2, n)
            char *s1, *s2;
            int n;

- *strcpy* — Copy string.
  - Synopsis: char *strcpy (s1, s2)
            char *s1, *s2;

- *strncpy* — Copy string up to *n* characters.
  - Synopsis: char *strncpy (s1, s2, n)
            char *s1, *s2;
            int n;

- *strlen* — Length of string.
  - Synopsis: int strlen (s)
            char *s;

- *strchr* — Search string for first occurrence of character.
  - Synopsis: char *strchr (s, c)
            char *s;
            int c;

- *strrchr* — Search string for last occurrence of character.
  - Synopsis: char *strrchr (s, c)
            char *s;
            int c;

- *strpbrk* — Search string for any one of a set of characters.
  - Synopsis: char *strpbrk (s1, s2)
                      char *s1, *s2;

- *strspn* — Length of initial string segment comprising characters in specified set.
  - Synopsis: int strspn (s1, s2)
                      char *s1, *s2;

- *strcspn* — Length of initial string segment comprising characters *not* in specified set.
  - Synopsis: int strcspn (s1, s2)
                      char *s1, *s2;

- *strtok* — Search string for tokens separated by any of a set of characters.
  - Synopsis: char *strtok (s1, s2)
                      char *s1, *s2;

CHARACTER TESTING

Manual Page — ctype(3C)

Note — The macros in this section are defined in **ctype.h**, which must be included whenever the macros are used by —
                      #include <ctype.h>

Synopsis: int name_of_macro (c)
                      int c;

isalpha	*c* is a letter.
isupper	*c* is an upper-case letter.
islower	*c* is a lower-case letter.
isdigit	*c* is a digit [0-9].
isxdigit	*c* is a hex digit [0-9], [A-F] or [a-f].
isalnum	*c* is an alphanumeric (letter or digit).
isspace	*c* is a Space, Tab, Carriage Return, Newline, Vertical Tab, or Formfeed.
ispunct	*c* is a punctuation character, that is, neither a control nor an alphanumeric character nor a Space.
isprint	*c* is a printing character, that is, ASCII codes 040 (Space) through 0176 (Tilde).
isgraph	*c* is a printing character other than Space.
iscntrl	*c* is a Delete character (0177) or a control character (0 through 037).
isascii	*c* is an ASCII character, that is, a code less than 0200.

CHARACTER TRANSLATION

Manual Page — All of the macros in this section are on the **conv(3C)** manual page.

Note — The macros in this section are defined in **ctype.h**, which must be included whenever the macros are used by —
> #include <ctype.h>

Synopsis: int name_of_macro (c)
> int c;

toascii Convert integer to ASCII character.
tolower Convert character to lowercase.
toupper Convert character to uppercase.
_tolower Same as **tolower**, but faster and more restricted.
_toupper Same as **toupper**, but faster and more restricted.

NUMERICAL CONVERSION

- **strtol** — Convert string to **long**.
  - Manual Page: strtol(3C)
  - Synopsis: long strtol (str, ptr, base)
    > char *str, **ptr;
    > int base;

- **atol** — Convert string to **long**. Special case of **strtol()**.
  - Manual Page: strtol(3C)
  - Synopsis: long atol (str)
    > char *str;

- **atoi** — Convert string to **int**. (**int**) type cast of **atol()**.
  - Manual Page: strtol(3C)
  - Synopsis: int atoi (str)
    > char *str;

- **atof** — Convert string to **double**.
  - Manual Page: strtod(3C)
  - Synopsis: double atof (str)
    > char *str;

- **strtod** — Convert string to **double**.
  - Manual Page: strtod(3C)
  - Synopsis: double strtod (str, ptr)
    > char *str, **ptr;

PARAMETER ACCESS

- *getenv* — Get string value associated with environment variable.
  - Manual Page: getenv(3C)
  - Synopsis: char *getenv (name)
        char *name;

- *getopt* — Get next option letter from argument list.
  - Manual Page: getopt(3C)
  - Synopsis: int getopt (argc, argv, optstring)
        int argc;
        char **argv, *opstring;

  The following **extern** variables are used to record the current argument pointer and index.
        extern char *optarg;
        extern int optind, opterr;

MEMORY ALLOCATION

Manual Page — All of the functions in this section are on the **malloc(3C)** page.

- *malloc* — Allocate memory.
  - Synopsis: char *malloc (size)
        unsigned size;

- *calloc* — Allocate memory and initialize to zeros.
  - Synopsis: char *calloc (nelem, elsize)
        unsigned nelem, elsize;

- *realloc* — Change size of previously allocated memory.
  - Synopsis: char *realloc (ptr, size)
        char *ptr;
        unsigned size;

- *free* — Free previously allocated memory.
  - Synopsis: void free (ptr)
        char *ptr;

FORMATTED OUTPUT
(printf, fprintf, sprintf)

INTRODUCTION

Legend

The following symbols are used in describing formatted output functions.

- *b*   Space. (*b* is *not* actually printed!)

- { }   Use only *one* of the listed elements.

- *[ ]*   Optional element. If two or more elements are listed, use only *one* of them, or *none*.

Notes

- To use functions in this section,
     #include <stdio.h>

- *printf, fprintf,* and *sprintf* are described in detail on the *printf(3S)* page of the *UNIX System V Programmer Reference Manual*.

- The *printf* functions can have a variable number of arguments. The number and type of arguments should match the conversion controls in the format string.

Synopses

- *printf* — Write using format to *stdout*.
  - Synopsis: int printf (format [,arg]...)
          char *format;

- *fprintf* — Write using format to specified stream.
  - Synopsis: int fprintf (stream, format [,arg]...)
          FILE *stream;
          char *format;

- *sprintf* — Place formatted string in character array.
  - Synopsis: int sprintf (s, format [,arg]...)
          char *s, format;

Example

printf ("error no. %d: %s", err, mesg);

- Prints *err* as a decimal integer and *mesg* as a string.

- Output would look like —
  error no. 13: cannot access file

CONVERSION CONTROL STRING

% [− for left justification] [width in characters or *] [type specific flags and parameters] conversion code

- **width** — Specifies the minimum number of character positions. The conversion result is **not** truncated if the width is too small.

- ***** — Width can be specified by a variable by using an ***** in place of width.

- **Example** —
  printf ("%*d", width, number);

CHARACTER CONTROL

% [−] [width] c

- **Examples** —
  - %c   A
  - %3c   ƀƀA
  - %−3c Aƀƀ

STRING CONTROL

% [−] [width] [.precision] s

- **precision** — Specifies the number of characters to be printed. If the string is longer than the precision, then the end of the string is truncated.

- **Examples** —
  - %10s   abcdefghijklmn
  - %−10.5s   abcdeƀƀƀƀƀ
  - %10.5s   ƀƀƀƀƀabcde

SIGNED INTEGER CONTROL

$\%\ \ [-]\ \begin{bmatrix} + \\ \cancel{b} \end{bmatrix}$ *[width] [l]   d*

- A minus (−) sign is automatically prepended to negative numbers. A + flag forces a + sign to be prepended to non-negative numbers; a ƀ flag forces a blank to be prepended.

- *Conversion codes —*
  l — Necessary for type *long*.
  d — Specifies signed decimal format for type *int*.

- *Examples —*
  - %d   43
  - %+d   +43
  - % d   ƀ43

UNSIGNED INTEGER CONTROL

$\%\ \ [-]\ \ [\#]\ \ [width]\ \ [l]\ \begin{Bmatrix} u \\ o \\ x \\ X \end{Bmatrix}$

- # — Forces a leading 0 to be prepended to octal format numbers, and 0x or 0X to be prepended to hexadecimal numbers.

- *l* — Necessary for type *long*.

- *Conversion codes —*
  u — Unsigned decimal
  o — Unsigned octal
  x — Unsigned hexadecimal
  X — Hexadecimal using uppercase letters

- *Examples* (32-bit integer) —
  - %u   777626577
  - %o   5626321721
  - %#o   05626321721
  - %x   2e59a3d1
  - %#X   0X2E59A3D1

FLOATING POINT CONTROL

$$\% \quad [-] \begin{bmatrix} + \\ b \end{bmatrix} [\#] \quad [width] \quad [.precision] \quad \begin{Bmatrix} f \\ e \\ E \\ g \\ G \end{Bmatrix}$$

- A minus (−) sign is automatically prepended to negative numbers. A + flag forces a + sign to be prepended to non-negative numbers; a *b* flag forces a blank to be prepended.

- Trailing 0's are not included unless a # flag is given. A # flag also forces a decimal point, even for 0 precision.

- *precision* — Specifies the number of digits to the right of the decimal point for *f*, *e*, and *E*; the number of significant digits for *g* and *G*. Rounding is done on truncation. The default precision is 6.

- *Conversion codes* —
  f [−]ddd.ddd
  e [−]d.dddde{±}dd
     (significant digits with exponent)
  E [−]d.ddddE{±}dd
  g Shorter of *f* and *e*
  G Shorter of *f* and *E*

- No distinction is made between *float* and *double* types.

- Floating point numbers are printed in decimal format.

- *Examples* —
  - %f   1234.567890
  - %.1f   1234.6
  - %E   1.234568E+03
  - %.3e   1.235e+03
  - %g   1234.57

LITERAL %

%%

- The only way to get a literal % is a control string.

- *Example* —
      printf ("%5.2f%%", 99.44)
      would print
      99.44%

FORMATTED INPUT
(scanf, fscanf, sscanf)

INTRODUCTION

Legend

The following symbols are used in describing formatted input functions.

- *b*   Space. (*b* is *not* actually printed!)
- { }   Use only *one* of the listed elements.
- [ ]   Optional element. If two or more elements are listed, use only *one* of them, or *none*.

Notes

- To use functions in this section,
             #include <stdio.h>

- *scanf, fscanf,* and *sscanf* are described in detail on the *scanf(3S)* page of the *UNIX System V Programmer Reference Manual*.

- The *scanf* functions can have a variable number of arguments. The numbers and types of arguments should match the conversion controls in the format string.

Synopses

- *scanf* — Read from *stdin* using format.
  - Synopsis: int scanf (format [,pointer]...)
             char *format;

- *fscanf* — Read from stream using format.
  - Synopsis: int fscanf (stream, format [,pointer]...)
             FILE *stream;
             char *format;

- *sscanf* — Read from string using format.
  - Synopsis: int sscanf (s, format [,pointer]...)
             char *s, *format;

Examples

- **input stream**

      12.45   1048.73   AE405271   438
- **scanf call**

      float x;   char id[8+1];   int n;
      scanf("%f%*f %8[A—Z0—9]%d", &x, id, &n);

  Assigns the **float** value **12.45** to **x**, skips **1048.73**, assigns the string **"AE405271"** to **id**, and **int** value **438** to **n**.

- **input stream**

      25 54.32E—01 monday
- **scanf call**

      int i; float x; char name[50];
      scanf ("%d%f%s", &i, &x, name);

  Assigns **25** to **i**, **5.432** to **x**, and **"monday"** to **name**.

- **input stream**

      56 789 0123 56ABC
- **scanf call**

      int i; float x; char name[50];
      scanf "%2d%f%*d,%[0—9]", &i, &x, name);

  Assigns **56** to **i and 789.0** to **x**, skips **0123**, and assigns **"56"** to **name**. The next call to **getchar** (see **getc (3S)** in the **UNIX System V Programmer Reference Manual**) would return ´**A**´.

CONVERSION CONTROL STRING

$$\% \quad [*] \quad [width] \quad \begin{bmatrix} type \\ specific \\ flags \end{bmatrix} \quad conversion\ code$$

- ***** — Causes the field to be skipped, that is, not assigned to a variable.

- **width** — Specifies the maximum field width in characters.

WHITESPACE

- In a format string, a Space or Tab character specifies one or more whitespace characters.

- In an input stream, whitespace characters (Space, Tab, Newline, Formfeed, Vertical Tab) are generally interpreted as field separators.

LITERAL CHARACTERS

- Literal characters in a format string, except Space, Tab, and %, require an exact match.

CHARACTER CONTROL

% [*] [width] c

- **width** — The number of characters specified by width is read and assigned to a character array. If width is omitted, then one character is read.

- Can be used to read a whitespace character.

STRING CONTROL

% [*] [width] s

- **width** — Specifies the maximum string length.

- In the input stream, strings are delimited by whitespace characters, and leading whitespace characters are ignored.

INTEGER CONTROL

$$\% \quad [*] \quad [width] \begin{bmatrix} l \\ h \end{bmatrix} \begin{Bmatrix} d \\ u \\ o \\ x \end{Bmatrix}$$

- *l* specifies type **long**, and *h* specifies **short**.
  The default is **int**.

- **Conversion codes** —
  d — Signed decimal
  u — Unsigned decimal
  o — Unsigned octal
  x — Unsigned hexadecimal

FLOATING POINT CONTROL

$$\% \quad [*] \quad [width] \quad [l] \begin{Bmatrix} f \\ e \\ g \end{Bmatrix}$$

- An *l* flag specifies **double** instead of **float**.

- *f*, *e*, and *g* are equivalent.

SCANSET

% [*] [width] scanset

- A scanset is specified by a list of characters enclosed by brackets.
  - *Examples* —
    - [abcd]
    - [A321]

- A contiguous (ASCII) range of characters can be specified using the first and last characters in the range.
  - *Examples* —
    - [a–z]
    - [A–F0–9]

- A ^ as the first character in a scanset specifies the complement of the set, that is, all characters except those specified.
  - *Example* —
    [^0–9]

- A scanset reads a string, including a terminating null character.

- Leading whitespace characters are *not* skipped.

GUIDE FOR WRITING
PORTABLE C PROGRAMS

INTRODUCTION

Portability is the goal — To write *C* programs that can be transferred from one machine to another running the *UNIX* operating system, with little or no change.

These are *guidelines*, not rules. There is no mechanical way to guarantee that a program will be portable. By keeping these guidelines in mind, you will write *C* programs that are *more portable* ... and are also *better organized* and thus are *easier to read, change*, and *maintain*.

USE lint (THE C PROGRAM CHECKER)

lint provides strong type checking, and shows many possibly nonportable constructions. If you use *lint* at *every stage* of a program's development, your program will be *easier to port* to another *UNIX* operating system. If you must rewrite an old program to make it portable, look at *lint* output, which will help you to identify trouble spots.

lint is a good aid for writing portable programs. However, *don't* assume that your program is automatically portable if it passes *lint*. Also, *don't* rely on *lint* to clean up poorly written programs, because it can miss some nonportable constructions. Instead, follow good programming practices such as those recommended in this guide.

See *lint* in *Section 1* of the *UNIX System V User Reference Manual*. Also see page 75 for another reference to *lint*.

DON'T USE COMPILER-DEPENDENT
FEATURES OF C

Certain details are *unspecified* in the *C* language definition. These details can cause small differences in different *C* compiler implementations. Though "small," these differences can cause problems when an attempt is made to port a program from one machine to another. For instance, the order of evaluation of function arguments is unspecified. Also, the order of evaluation of operands of most binary operators, such as addition or multiplication, is unspecified (see page 19 for a discussion of this). The order of any possible side effects from these operands is therefore *unknown*. Thus you should *not* rely on unspecified features of the language.

DON'T USE MACHINE-DEPENDENT FEATURES OF C

Don't depend on the machine's word size.

- The size of an *int* type depends on the machine's word size, which *varies* on different machines. If you are uncertain of the result of an integer operation, use *long*s to avoid potential overflow problems.

- There is *no* guarantee that an *int* is the size of a machine word. All that is specified by the *C* language definition is that the size of a *short* is less than or equal to the size of an *int*, which is less than or equal to the size of a *long*.

- Word size can affect constants such as bit masks.
  - *Example* —

    ```
    ...
    #define MASK 0177770    /* WRONG */
    int x;
    x &= MASK;
    ...
    ```

    The above will clear the 3 *right*most bits of *x* correctly, *only* when an *int* is 16 bits in size. On the other hand, the *left*most bits of *x* will be cleared when an *int* has more than 16 bits. To avoid these problems, use this *#define* instead —

    ```
    ...
    #define MASK (~07)    /* RIGHT */
    int x;
    x &= MASK;
    ...
    ```

    This example works on *all* machines *regardless* of the size of an *int*.

Examine shift operations carefully.

- The maximum number of bits that can be shifted left or right *varies* on different machines. If you shift more than the maximum allowed, you will get unexpected results.

- Cast integer quantities to *unsigned* before shifting, if there is any possibility of trouble. On some machines, shifts are done logically; vacated bits are replaced by 0 bits. On other machines, arithmetic shifts are performed and vacated bits are replaced by a copy of the sign bit. However, *unsigned* quantities are *guaranteed* by the *C* language definition to be shifted *logically*.

Use #define to define numeric constants as symbolic constants.

- It is poor programming practice to use numeric constants, especially when their meaning is not immediately obvious. Numeric constants are better represented by **symbolic** constants associated with them by **#define**. This method also lets you find these definitions more easily if you **store them in a standard place**, such as at the beginning of a program or in a header file.

- **Example —**
  ...
  #define SCREENWIDTH 80
  ...
  This allows you to use **SCREENWIDTH** in place of **80**.

Use the sizeof operator to refer to the size of the object.

- A constant is often used to represent the size of some object. But such usage is **not** portable. Use the **sizeof** operator instead.

- **Example —**
  ...
  #define NUMELEM(ARRAY) \
    (sizeof(ARRAY) / sizeof(*(ARRAY)))
  ...
  This yields the number of elements in an array in a portable way.

Don't use multicharacter character constants.

- Because character constants are really objects of type **int**, the **C** language definition allows multicharacter character constants. However, the order in which the characters are assigned in a word **varies** on different machines.

Don't depend on the internal representation of integers.

- Most machines represent integers in **two's complement** notation; others use **one's complement** notation. Therefore, **don't** write code that takes advantage of two's complement notation. For example, left shifting a negative integer value by 1 bit to multiply it by 2 does **not** work on a one's complement machine.

Remember that floating point representations and accuracy vary on different machines.

- Floating point numbers have *different* internal representations on different machines. Therefore, results from programs using floating point arithmetic may have *different* accuracy on different machines. *Avoid*, or at least *highlight*, dependence on a particular format.

Don't depend on the number of bytes in a word. Don't depend on the order of bytes within a word.

- The number of bytes in a word, and the order of bytes within a word, *varies* on different machines.

- *Example* —
  In the following *incorrect* function, a null character will be written if the low order byte is not the lowest address byte in *c* —

  ```
  ...
  #define STDOUT1
  putchar(c)   /* WRONG */
  int c;
  {
     write(STDOUT, (char *) &c, 1);
  }
  ...
  ```
  In the above example, *c* should, of course, be declared as a *char* and the cast need *not* be done.

Don't depend on the number of bits in a byte.

- Because the number of bits in a byte *varies* on different machines, you can*not* assume that bytes are always 8-bit quantities. To find out the number of bits in a byte, use the symbolic constant kept in the standard header file */usr/include/values.h*.

- *Note* — All system header files available to the programmer are kept in the */usr/include* directory.

Be careful when using signed character quantities.

- On some machines, *chars* are signed quantities. As a result, in expressions, *chars* are sign-extended when evaluated. In some cases, you may use *unsigned char* variables or cast characters to *unsigned char* to make character variables portable. In other cases, you may have to use some type other than *char*.

- *Example* —
  There is a danger that a subscript could index *before* the beginning of the table on a machine with signed characters —
  ```
  ...
  #define TABSIZE 256
  char c;
  extern char table[TABSIZE]
  c = table[c];   /* WRONG */
  ...
  ```
  To avoid this possibility, either declare *c* as an *unsigned char*, or cast the subscript to *unsigned char*.

- *Example* —
  The following *incorrect* code fragment will *never* detect end-of-file on machines that have only unsigned characters —
  ```
  ...
  #include <stdio.h>
  char c;        /* WRONG */
  if ((c = getchar()) != EOF)
  ...
  ```
  On machines where *chars* are unsigned, the value of *c* will *never* be equal to EOF that is defined as −1. The library function *getchar* (page 49) yields an *int*, so you should declare *c* to be an *int*.

Don't combine separate bit fields.
Don't use bit fields to represent external data layouts.

- You can make bit fields *portable*, if you *don't* combine separate bit fields. This is because the maximum size of a bit field depends on the machine's word size, and bit fields cannot straddle word boundaries. Also, the allocation order of bit fields in a word is machine-dependent — either left-to-right, or right-to-left.

- Using bit fields to represent external data layouts makes a program *non*portable. To minimize problems, place bit field templates in header files and label them as machine-dependent.

Use casts for pointer conversions.

- In general, pointer conversions are *not* portable. However, you can convert a pointer to any integer type that is large enough to hold it, and set it back to yielding the original pointer. Also, a pointer to an object can be cast to a pointer to a smaller object and back again without change.

Watch out for alignment restrictions when dereferencing pointers.

- If you convert a pointer of one type to a pointer of another type, your program may cause an addressing exception when the converted pointer is dereferenced. This is caused by restrictions on machine alignment. Use library function *malloc* (page 55) to return a character pointer to a storage area that is suitably aligned, so that this pointer can be cast to any pointer type.

Watch out for signed pointer comparisons.

- Some machines do *signed* pointer comparisons ... others do *unsigned* comparisons. This difference does not cause problems if you are comparing pointers generated from valid addresses. Assigning −1 to a pointer may give either the largest possible pointer value, or a value that is smaller than any valid pointer value.

- The only "safe" constant that can be assigned to a pointer is 0, when 0 is cast to the pointer type.

Watch out for pointer wraparound.

- Pointer arithmetic may cause overflow or underflow. This pointer wraparound effect might occur if an object such as an array were near the end or beginning of memory.

- *Example* —
  This code fragment is an example where pointer underflow can occur.
  ```
  ...
  struct large x[SIZE], *p;  /* WRONG */
  for (p = x[SIZE−1]; p >= x; p−−)
  ...
  ```
  If the array *x* resides at a low memory address, then it is possible that x−1 is *not less* than *x*, but is *greater* than *x* because of pointer wraparound.

Don't depend on a particular character set.

- *Don't* write code that assumes that the character set has a contiguous collating sequence.
  - *Example* —
    ```
    ...
    char c;
    if (c >= 'a' && c <= 'z')    /* WRONG */
    ...
    ```
    This checks to see if *c* is a lowercase letter in a *non*portable way. The *portable* way to do this check is —
    ```
    ...
    char c;
    if (islower(c))    /* RIGHT */
    ...
    ```
    The library function *islower* (page 53) should be defined elsewhere and marked machine-dependent. Such action makes this test portable because the specification of the above test is portable.

- Be aware that different character sets may have a *different* number of characters in them.

- *Don't* take the difference between two letters to calculate how far apart they are in the character set.

Don't use programming tricks that depend on hardware.

- Any slight boost in efficiency in your program derived when you write code for a particular machine may not be worth the loss of portability.

DESIGN WELL ORGANIZED PROGRAMS

A well organized program is easier to *read, change,* and *maintain* ... and therefore to *port*.

Use header files to contain environment-specific and hardware-dependent information.

- Two important features for writing portable programs are the *#include* and *#define* macros of the preprocessor (page 39). Put definitions of data types, symbolic constants, and macro definitions shared by more than one program in a single header file, so that any changes can be made in one place.
  - *Example —*

    ```
    ...
    #include <values.h>
    ...
    ```

    The above statement includes the standard header file */usr/include/values.h*, which contains system-wide hardware constants.

- Use header files for common definitions of a project, that is, a set of related programs. Similarly, use local header files for individual programs.

- Use header files to isolate data and environment-dependent data such as filenames or options. Place anything that can vary across systems, or even within the same system, in header files where it can be easily located and modified.

- *Don't* place external variable definitions that allocate storage, in header files. Use header files *solely* for preprocessor definitions and for type definitions.

Use functions, conditional compilations, and #define macros to isolate machine-dependent code.

- Write separate machine-dependent functions and place them in their own source files. If there are several such source files, keep them in a *separate directory*.

- Surround machine-dependent sections of code with conditional compilation statements of the preprocessor (page 40).
  - *Example —*
    The following section of code shows where a stack pointer grows in different directions, due to physical machine characteristics.

    ```
    ...
        int *stackptr;
    #ifdef MACHINE1
        *--stackptr = datum;  /* grows down */
    #else
        *++stackptr = datum;  /* grows up */
    #endif
    ...
    ```

- Macros using the *#define* macro (page 39) can be written to hide machine-dependent features.
  - *Example —*

    ```
    ...
    #define BITSPERBYTE 8
    #define BITS(TYPE) \
        (sizeof(TYPE) * BITSPERBYTE)
    ...
    ```

    The specification of the *constant* named *BITSPERBYTE* is *portable*, the implementation is *not*. *Both* the specification and implementation of the *macro* named *BITS* are *portable*.

Be sure to supply to functions the correct number of arguments having the right type.

- Ensure that arguments used in calls to functions agree in number and in type with the function's formal arguments. Even if you can pass fewer arguments, *don't leave any out*. Instead, pass some dummy values, such as nulls.

- A facility in */usr/include/varargs.h* allows you to define a function with a variable number of arguments in a portable way. For example, library function *printf* (page 56) is implemented with the *varargs* mechanism. *Note —* See *varargs* in *Section 5* of the *UNIX System V Programmer Reference Manual*.

Call the system via standard library functions when possible, instead of doing your own system calls.

- The standard *UNIX* system library functions, described in *Section 3* of the *UNIX System V Programmer Reference Manual*, provide a large assortment of standard functions of general use. Included are standard library functions that provide operating system services, such as input and output operations. These functions provide an extra degree of portability because they insulate your programs from any possible system changes. *Note* — Also see pages 46-63 of this handbook.

Define external names carefully.

- To enhance the maintainability and portability of your program, keep all *external variable definitions* of a program *in their own source file*. Note that all other source files of your program refer to those global variables by *extern* declarations (pages 35 and 38). You have a choice of methods. You can place these external declarations *at the top of the program source files* (presumably as the result of file inclusion), or you can *declare within the function* those external variables required by the function.

- The maximum number of significant characters for external variables and functions depends on the operating system environment. In addition, some systems fold all lowercase letters to uppercase. Linker programs will complain about conflicts but will *not* always detect unintended clashes of names, so *don't* depend on the linker to find conflicts.

Use typedef declarations to hide machine-dependent data types.

- The *typedef* declaration (page 33) provides a means of hiding machine-dependent data types. If you change the *typedef* declaration, all variables defined by the *typedef* will change correspondingly. The system provides you with a set of standard system *typedefs* in header file */usr/include/sys/types.h*.

- *Example* —

      ...
      typedef unsigned short ino_t; /* inode number */
      ...

  The above is an example of some of the *typedef* uses in a typical */usr/include/sys/types.h*.

PORTABILITY OF DATA FILES

Use character input/output to move binary data files.

- Binary data files are inherently **non**portable because different machines use **different** internal representations of data objects. Unfortunately, there is no simple way to move data files. Byte order differences can create serious problems in machine-to-machine communication if integer information is transmitted on a byte-by-byte basis. Also, character sets are **not** standard for all machines.

- One approach is to write special conversion programs that "know" about the exact format of the data. Another approach is to write bytes in a data object in some machine-independent order and then read them back in on the other machine in that same order. Use library functions **printf** and **scanf** (pages 56 and 60) to transmit data using **character** rather than binary input/output, unless that is impractical.

REFERENCES AND SUGGESTED READING

S. C. Johnson, "LINT, A C Program Checker," *UNIX System Programmer's Manual, Volume 2*, AT&T Bell Laboratories. Published by Holt, Rinehart, and Winston, New York, 1983, 1979. Pages 278-290.

S. C. Johnson and D. M. Ritchie, "UNIX Time-Sharing System: Portability of C Programs and the UNIX System," *The Bell System Technical Journal,* July-August 1978, (Volume 57, No. 6, Part 2), pages 2021-2048. AT&T Bell Laboratories, Murray Hill, NJ 07974.

B. W. Kernighan and D. M. Ritchie, *The C Programming Language,* Prentice-Hall, Englewood Cliffs, NJ, 1978.

T. Plum, *C Programming Guidelines*, Plum-Hall, Cardiff, NJ, 1984.

ASCII CHARACTER SET

Note — ^@, ^A, etc. indicate *CTRL/@, CTRL/A,* etc. This character set may differ slightly on different terminals.

CONTROL CHARACTERS

Dec	Oct	Hex	ASCII
0	000	00	^@ NUL (Null)
1	001	01	^A SOH (Start of Heading)
2	002	02	^B STX (Start Text)
3	003	03	^C ETX (End Text)
4	004	04	^D EOT (End of Transmission)
5	005	05	^E ENQ (Enquiry)
6	006	06	^F ACK (Acknowledge)
7	007	07	^G BEL (Bell)
8	010	08	^H BS (Backspace)
9	011	09	^I TAB HT (Horizontal Tab)
10	012	0A	^J LF (Linefeed, Newline)
11	013	0B	^K VT (Vertical Tab)
12	014	0C	^L FF (Formfeed)
13	015	0D	^M CR (Carriage Return)
14	016	0E	^N SO (Shift Out)
15	017	0F	^O SI (Shift In)
16	020	10	^P DLE (Data Link Escape)
17	021	11	^Q DC1 (X-ON)
18	022	12	^R DC2
19	023	13	^S DC3 (X-OFF)
20	024	14	^T DC4
21	025	15	^U NAK (Negative Acknowledge)
22	026	16	^V SYN (Synchronous Idle)
23	027	17	^W ETB (End Transmission Blocks)
24	030	18	^X CAN (Cancel)
25	031	19	^Y EM (End of Medium)
26	032	1A	^Z SUB (Substitute)
27	033	1B	^[ESC (Escape)
28	034	1C	^\ FS (File Separator)
29	035	1D	^] GS (Group Separator)
30	036	1E	^^ RS (Record Separator)
31	037	1F	^_ US (Unit Separator)

SPACE

Dec	Oct	Hex	ASCII
32	040	20	SPACEBAR SP (Space)

PRINTING CHARACTERS

Dec	Oct	Hex	ASCII	Dec	Oct	Hex	ASCII
33	041	21	!	81	121	51	Q
34	042	22	"	82	122	52	R
35	043	23	#	83	123	53	S
36	044	24	$	84	124	54	T
37	045	25	%	85	125	55	U
38	046	26	&	86	126	56	V
39	047	27	'	87	127	57	W
40	050	28	(	88	130	58	X
41	051	29	)	89	131	59	Y
42	052	2A	*	90	132	5A	Z
43	053	2B	+	91	133	5B	[
44	054	2C	,	92	134	5C	\
45	055	2D	—	93	135	5D	]
46	056	2E	.	94	136	5E	^
47	057	2F	/	95	137	5F	_
48	060	30	0	96	140	60	`
49	061	31	1	97	141	61	a
50	062	32	2	98	142	62	b
51	063	33	3	99	143	63	c
52	064	34	4	100	144	64	d
53	065	35	5	101	145	65	e
54	066	36	6	102	146	66	f
55	067	37	7	103	147	67	g
56	070	38	8	104	150	68	h
57	071	39	9	105	151	69	i
58	072	3A	:	106	152	6A	j
59	073	3B	;	107	153	6B	k
60	074	3C	<	108	154	6C	l
61	075	3D	=	109	155	6D	m
62	076	3E	>	110	156	6E	n
63	077	3F	?	111	157	6F	o
64	100	40	@	112	160	70	p
65	101	41	A	113	161	71	q
66	102	42	B	114	162	72	r
67	103	43	C	115	163	73	s
68	104	44	D	116	164	74	t
69	105	45	E	117	165	75	u
70	106	46	F	118	166	76	v
71	107	47	G	119	167	77	w
72	110	48	H	120	170	78	x
73	111	49	I	121	171	79	y
74	112	4A	J	122	172	7A	z
75	113	4B	K	123	173	7B	{
76	114	4C	L	124	174	7C		
77	115	4D	M	125	175	7D	}
78	116	4E	N	126	176	7E	~
79	117	4F	O				
80	120	50	P	127	177	7F	DEL, RUB

INDEX

Note — Also see *INDEX TO LIBRARY FUNCTIONS* and *INDEX TO OPERATORS* on the *Outside Back Cover*.

A

Address Operators ... 16
ar Command ... 2
argc, argv Parameters (Functions) ... 28
Arithmetic Conversions ... 19
Arithmetic Operators ... 10
Array Operators ... 16
Arrays (Initialization) (Declarations) ... 36
Arrays, Pointers and (Declarations) ... 30
ASCII Character Set ... 76
asm Statement ... 4
Assignment Operators ... 12
Assignment Statement ... 20
Associativity, Precedence and ... 18
automatic (Defining a Variable) (Declarations) ... 33

B

Backslash (\) ... 39
Basic Data Types ... 4, 5
Basic Type Declarations ... 29
Basic Types (Initialization) (Declarations) ... 36
bblsort.c (Program Structure) ... 44
bblsort.h and *main.c* (Program Structure) ... 42
Bell System Technical Journal ... 75
Bit Fields in Structures — *struct* (Declarations) ... 31
Bitwise Operators ... 15
Block, Compound Statement ... 20
Block, Defining a Variable Within a ... 33
Block I/O (I/O Library) ... 50
Boolean Operators ... 14
break Statement ... 21

C

C Programming Guidelines ... 75
C Programming Language ... 75
CAI *UNIX* System Courses ... 2
Call, Function ... 27
case Statement ... 23
cc Command ... 2
char Data Type ... 5, 7, 29
Character Constants ... 7
Character Control (Formatted Input) ... 62
Character Control (Formatted Output) ... 57
Character Set, ASCII ... 76
Character Testing (Other Libraries) ... 53
Character Translation (Other Libraries) ... 54
Characters, Legal ... 3
Classes, Storage ... 4
Commands, Useful ... 2
Comments ... 3
Compiler-Dependent Features of *C*, Don't Use ... 64
Compound Statement (Block) ... 20
Computer-Assisted Instruction *UNIX* System Courses ... 2
Conditional Compilation (Preprocessor) ... 40
Constants ... 5, 6, 7
continue Statement ... 21
Conversion Control String (Formatted Input) ... 61
Conversion Control String (Formatted Output) ... 57
Conversions, Arithmetic ... 19
Courses on the *UNIX* System ... 2

D

Data Files, Portability of ... 74
Data Sizes, Hardware Dependent ... 8
Data Types, Basic ... 4, 5
Declaration of Parameters (Functions) ... 26
Declarations ... 29
Declaring Objects Defined Elsewhere (Declarations) ... 38
default Statement ... 23
#define (Preprocessor) ... 39
Defining a Variable (Declarations) ... 33, 35
Definition, Function ... 26
Design Well Organized Programs ... 71
do...while Statement ... 24
Documentation, *UNIX* System ... 2
double Data Type ... 5, 6, 29

E

#else (Preprocessor) ... 40
else Statement ... 22
#endif (Preprocessor) ... 40
enum (Declarations) ... 32
Enumeration Constants ... 7
Enumerations — **enum** (Declarations) ... 32
env Parameter (Functions) ... 28
Evaluation Order, Operand ... 19
Executing Another Program (Other Libraries) ... 51
Expression Statements ... 20
Expressions, Operators and ... 9
extern Declaration ... 35, 38
External Identifiers ... 3
External Level, Defining a Variable (Declarations) ... 35

F

File Access (I/O Library) ... 47
File Inclusion (Preprocessor) ... 39
File Name, Line Number and (Preprocessor) ... 40
File Status (I/O Library) ... 48
float Data Type ... 5, 6, 29
Floating Point Constants ... 6
Floating Point Control (Formatted Input) ... 62
Floating Point Control (Formatted Output) ... 59
for Statement ... 25
Formal Parameter (Defining a Variable) (Declarations) ... 34
Format ... 3
Format and Nesting (Statement) ... 20
Formatted Input ... 60
Formatted I/O (I/O Library) ... 48
Formatted Output ... 56
Formfeeds, Spaces, Tabs, Newlines ... 3
fortran Statement ... 4
fprintf Function ... 56
fscanf Function ... 60
Function Call ... 27
Function Call Statement ... 20
Function Definition ... 26
Function Name ... 26
Functions ... 26

G

General Syntax ... 3
Global (Defining a Variable) (Declarations) ... 35
goto Statement ... 21
Guide for Writing Portable C Programs ... 64

H

Hardware Dependent Data Sizes ... 8

I

Identifiers ... 3
Identifiers, External ... 3
#if (Preprocessor) ... 40
if Statement ... 22
if...else Statement ... 22
#ifdef (Preprocessor) ... 40
#ifndef (Preprocessor) ... 40
#include (Preprocessor) ... 39
Initialization (Declarations) ... 36
Input, Formatted ... 60
Instructor-Led *UNIX* System Courses ... 2
int Data Type ... 5, 29
Integer Constants ... 5
Integer Control (Formatted Input) ... 62
I/O Library ... 46, Index on Outside Back Cover

J

Johnson, S.C., "LINT, A C Program Checker" ... 75
Johnson, S.C., and D.M. Ritchie, "Portability of C Programs" ... 75

K

Kernighan, B.W., and D.M. Ritchie,
  The C Programming Language ... 75
Keywords, Reserved ... 4

L

Label, Statement ... 20
Legal Characters ... 3
Libraries, Other ... 51, Index on Outside Back Cover
Library Functions Index ... Outside Back Cover
Library, I/O ... 46, Index on Outside Back Cover
Line Number and File Name (Preprocessor) ... 40
#line (Preprocessor) ...40
lint Command ... 2, 27, 64, 75
Literal Characters (Formatted Input) ... 62
Literal % (Formatted Output) ... 59
long Data Type ... 5, 6, 29
Long Integer Constants ... 6

M

Machine-Dependent Features of *C*, Don't Use ... 65
Macros (Preprocessor) ... 39
main Function ... 28
main.c, bblsort.h and (Program Structure) ... 42
make Command ... 2
Memory Allocation (Other Libraries) ... 55
Miscellaneous Operators ... 17

N

Nesting, Format and (Statement) ... 20
Newlines, Formfeeds, Spaces, Tabs ... 3
Notation, Operand ... 9
Null Statement ... 20
Numerical Conversion (Other Libraries) ... 54

O

Operand Evaluation Order ... 19
Operand Notation ... 9
Operators and Expressions ... 9
Operators Chart and Index ... 18, Outside Back Cover
Other Libraries ... 51, Index on Outside Back Cover
Output, Formatted ... 56

P

Parameter Access (Other Libraries) ... 55
Parameter List (Functions) ... 26
Pipe Access (I/O Library) ... 48
Plum, T., *C Programming Guidelines* ... 75
Pointers and Arrays (Declarations) ... 30
Portability ... 64
Precedence and Associativity ... 18
Preprocessor ... 39
printf Function ... 56
Program Structure ... 41

R

References and Suggested Reading ... 75
register (Defining a Variable) (Declarations) ... 34
Relational Operators ... 13
Renaming a Type — *typedef* (Declarations) ... 33
Reserved Keywords ... 4
return expression Statement ... 21
return Statement ... 21
Returned Value (Functions) ... 26
Ritchie, D.M., and B. W. Kernighan,
   The C Programming Language ... 75
Ritchie, D.M., and S.C. Johnson, "Portability of C Programs" ... 75

S

scanf Function ... 60
scanset (Formatted Input) ... 63
sdb Command ... 2
short Data Type ... 5, 29
Side Effects (++ and −−) ... 11
Signed Integer Control (Formatted Output) ... 58
Single Character I/O — Input (I/O Library) ... 49
Single Character I/O — Output (I/O Library) ... 50
sizeof Operator ... 17
Spaces, Tabs, Newlines, Formfeeds ... 3
Special Character Constants ... 7
sprintf Function ... 56
sscanf Function ... 60
Statement Label ... 20
Statements ... 4, 20
static (Defining a Variable) (Declarations) ... 34, 35
stdio.h (I/O Library) ... 46
Storage Classes ... 4
String Constants ... 7
String Control (Formatted Input) ... 62
String Control (Formatted Output) ... 57
String I/O (I/O Library) ... 49
String Manipulation (Other Libraries) ... 52
Strings (Initialization) (Declarations) ... 36
struct (Declarations) ... 31
Structure/Union Operators ... 16
Structures — *struct* (Declarations) ... 31
Structures, Bit Fields in (Declarations) ... 31
Structures (Initialization) (Declarations) ... 37
Suggested Reading, References and ... 75
switch Statement ... 23
Syntax, General ... 3
System Header Files, */usr/include* ... 67

T

Tabs, Newlines, Formfeeds, Spaces ... 3
Temporary Files (Other Libraries) ... 51
Token Replacement (Preprocessor) ... 39
Type, Renaming a (Declarations) ... 33
typedef (Declarations) ... 4, 33

U

#undef (Preprocessor) ... 39
union (Declarations) ... 32
Union, Structure Operators ... 16
UNIX System Courses and Documentation ... 2
unsigned Data Type ... 5, 29
Unsigned Integer Control (Formatted Output) ... 58
Useful Commands ... 2
/usr/include System Header Files ... 67

V

varargs Macros ... 72
Variable, Defining a (Declarations) ... 33, 35
void Data Type ... 26, 29, 38

W

while Statement ... 24
Whitespace (Formatted Input) ... 61